Usborne Beginners
Planes

Fiona Patchett
Designed by Nicola Butler

Additional design by Michelle Lawrence

Illustrated by Colin King, Mark Ruffle and Ian McNee

Planes consultant: L.F.E. Coombs

Reading consultant: Alison Kelly

Contents

Busy airports

Lots of planes fly to different places around the world.

These planes are getting ready to fly.

A closer look

This plane is a jumbo jet. It can carry over 400 passengers.

The plane is made of strong, light metal.

Wing

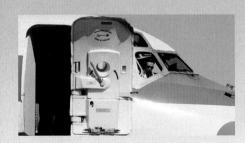

The captain sits in the cockpit at the front of the plane.

In the cabin, there are about 68 rows of seats for passengers.

The shape of the
wings and the tail help
the plane to fly.

—Tail

—Engine

Jumbo jets have four powerful engines,
which make the plane fly.

Jumbo jets are the largest
passenger planes. Even larger planes
carry things such as food or mail.

At the airport

Airports are very busy places. Lots of people help get every plane ready to fly.

Passengers wait inside a terminal building.

A ground crew gets the plane ready.

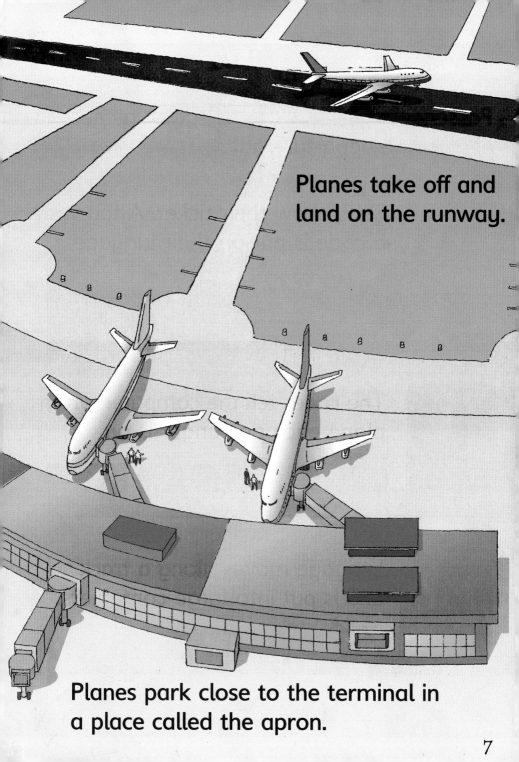

Planes take off and land on the runway.

Planes park close to the terminal in a place called the apron.

Checking in

Passengers leave their luggage at a check-in desk in the departure hall.

They show their ticket. A tag with a code is put on their luggage.

The codes tell the computer which plane each passenger is on.

Luggage moves along a track and is put into large containers.

Animals travel in their own containers.

At check-in they are given their own tags.

Some big animals travel to zoos or parks by plane.

Can you see the elephant's trunk?

Some airlines let you store your pet under your seat on the plane.

Security checks

Passengers are checked to make sure they do not take anything dangerous on the plane.

Passengers show their passport or identification card.

They walk through a security gate.

If they are carrying anything made of metal, an alarm goes off.

Everything passengers carry must go through an x-ray machine.

The shapes of things in each bag show on a screen.

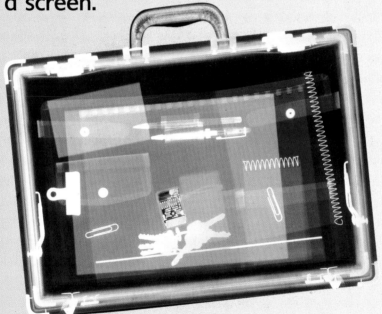

Can you see the keys and paperclips in this case?

Passengers then wait in a departure lounge until their plane is ready.

Getting ready

The plane is filled with fuel which is stored in the wings of the plane.

BP

Fuel truck

There are tanks of fuel under the runway. A truck pumps the fuel into the plane.

Plane fuel is either clear or pink!

The captain checks the weather and plans the route.

A computer helps him work out how much fuel is needed.

The engines are checked to make sure they work properly and that the plane is safe to fly.

Loading the plane

Luggage, food and drink
are loaded onto the plane.

A truck lifts a trailer full of ready-made
meals up to the plane.

The food is wheeled
onto the plane.

It is stored in kitchens,
called galleys.

Sometimes, a few cars travel with the luggage.

A truck lifts containers of luggage up to the plane. The containers are stored in a large area under the cabin.

AKE 12400 IR

Waiting to fly

After the passengers have boarded the plane, the captain waits his turn to take off.

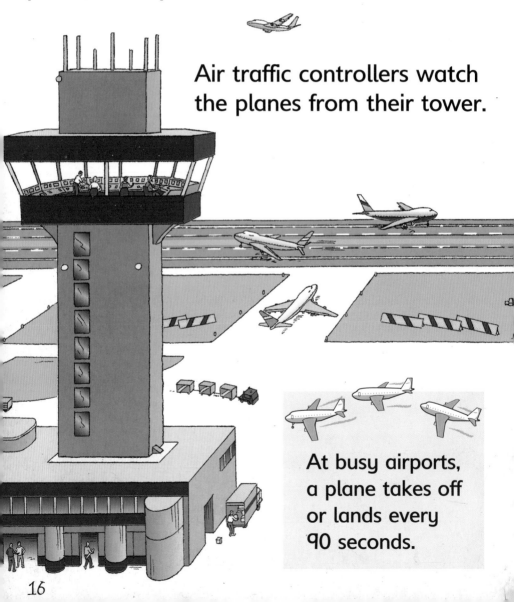

Air traffic controllers watch the planes from their tower.

At busy airports, a plane takes off or lands every 90 seconds.

A controller can see the planes near the airport on screens.

She contacts the captain when it is safe to move the plane.

The captain and co-pilot use computers and controls to help them fly the plane.

Taking off

The captain moves the plane to the runway and gets ready for take off.

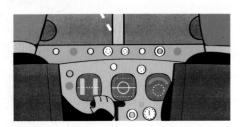

The captain pushes the levers. The plane moves very fast.

He pulls the control column. The plane lifts off the ground.

A plane travels down a runway faster than a racing car.

The wheels fold up under the plane.

The tops of the wings are curved. Air moves very fast over them.

The air moves so fast that the plane is sucked upward.

Above the clouds

The plane flies higher and higher.

On a long flight, the captain uses a computer, called the autopilot, to fly instead of him.

He presses some buttons to switch on the autopilot.

Either the captain or the co-pilot must stay in the cockpit.

The air above the clouds is six times colder than the inside of a freezer.

Above the clouds, the flight is less bumpy.

Changing direction

Air traffic controllers tell the captain if the plane needs to change direction.

Parts of the wings and tail move to make the plane turn in the air.

A jumbo jet is as heavy as 100 elephants, but it can fly like a bird.

The captain keeps in touch with different air traffic controllers along the route.

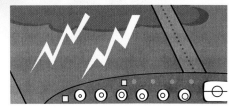

If there is a storm ahead, they tell him to change direction.

Planes can fly through storms, but the flight is bumpy.

Landing

Near the airport where the plane is going to land, air traffic controllers contact the captain.

The plane flies lower and flaps under the wings move to help the plane fly slower.

The wheels come down, with a clunk.

An air traffic controller tells the captain when to land.

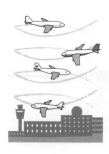

At busy airports, planes fly around and around before they can land.

The plane flies close to the runway and lands.

The captain puts on the brakes to slow the plane down, then steers it to the apron.

Another flight

The ground crew guide the plane to the terminal with bright discs, cones or sticks.

In less than one hour, the plane needs to be ready for another flight.

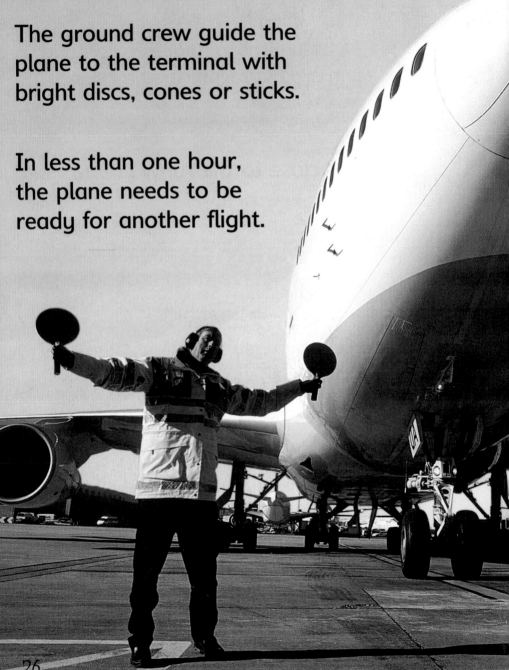

 Passengers collect their luggage from the terminal.

 The plane is cleaned and refuelled. New luggage is loaded.

 Another captain and co-pilot get ready for the next flight.

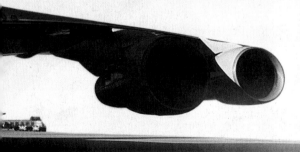

When the plane stops, blocks are put in front of the wheels. They stop the plane from rolling.

Other planes

Planes come in lots of different shapes and sizes.

Stealth fighter planes have a triangle shaped body and two pointed tail fins.

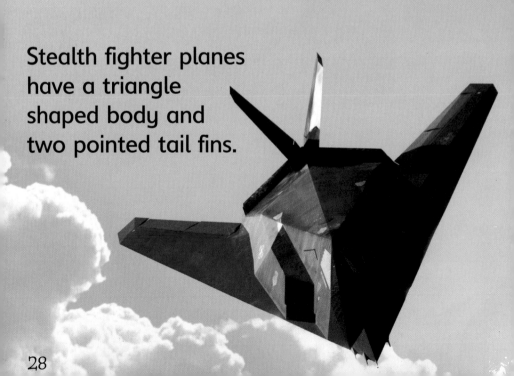

Concorde is the fastest passenger plane.

This jetliner is much smaller than a jumbo. It has two engines and only carries ten passengers.

Engine

Seaplanes take off and land on the sea.

They use calm water for a runway.

They land on floats instead of wheels.

Glossary of plane words

Here are some of the words in this book you might not know. This page tells you what they mean.

 cockpit - computers and controls which help the captain fly the plane.

 terminal - the building at an airport where passengers wait for their plane.

 runway - the part of an airport where planes take off and land.

 apron - an area close to the terminal where planes park.

 galley - a kitchen on a plane where ready-made meals are stored.

 x-ray machine - a machine which shows what passengers are carrying.

 air traffic controllers - people on the ground who help the captain.

Web sites to visit

If you have a computer, you can find out more about planes on the Internet. On the Usborne Quicklinks Web site there are links to four fun Web sites.

Web site 1 - Do a quiz and watch a short movie about planes.

Web site 2 - Find out how planes work.

Web site 3 - Do a wordsearch and make some paper planes.

Web site 4 - Fill in some pictures of different planes.

To visit these Web sites, go to **www.usborne-quicklinks.com** and type the keywords "beginners planes". Then, click on the link for the Web site you want to visit. Before you use the Internet, look at the safety guidelines inside the back cover of this book and ask an adult to read them with you.

Index

Acknowledgements

Managing editor: Fiona Watt, Managing designer: Mary Cartwright
Photographic manipulation by John Russell
With thanks to John Armstrong and Katie Daynes

Photo credits

The publishers are grateful to the following for permission to reproduce material.
Cover George Hall/CORBIS **p1** © 1997 John M. Dibbs/The Plane Picture Company. **p2-3** © 1997 John
M. Dibbs/The Plane Picture Company. **p4 (left)** Steve Raymer/CORBIS. **p4 (right)** Fabrizio Fresia.
p4-5 Thomas Fischer. **p9** © Anthony Bannister; Gallo Images/CORBIS. **p11** Lester Lefkowitz/CORBIS.
p12 © Mark Wagner/Aviation-Images.com. **p13** © Mark Wagner/Aviation-Images.com. **p14** The Flight
Collection/R.Shaw. **p15** BAA/Anthony Charlton. **p17** The Flight Collection/Jeremy Hoare. **p18-19**
Pictures Colour Library Ltd. **p20-21** © 1997 John M. Dibbs/The Plane Picture Company. **p22-23** Colin
K. Work. **p25** Colin K. Work. **p26-27** BAA/Anthony Charlton. **p28** GettyImages/Ross Harrison Koty.
p28-29 The Flight Collection. **p29** Colin K. Work. **p31** © Mark Wagner/Aviation-Images.com.